D1307854

Daily Life

The American Colonies

Jeanne DuPrau

KidHaven Press

KidHaven Press, an imprint of Gale Group, Inc.

P.O. Box 289009, San Diego, CA 92198-9009

Library of Congress Cataloging-in-Publication Data

DuPrau, Jeanne.
    The American colonies / by Jeanne DuPrau.
       p. cm. — (Daily life)
    Includes bibliographical references.
    ISBN 0-7377-0936-7 (hardback : alk. paper)
    1. United States—Social life and customs—To 1775—Juvenile
literature. 2. United States—History—Colonial period, ca.
1600–1775—Juvenile literature. I. Title. II. Series.
    E162 .D87 2002
    973.2—dc21

    2001002185

Picture Credits

Cover: © James R. Bingham/Wood River/PictureQuest
© Archive Photos, 13
© William A. Bake/CORBIS, 16
© Annie Griffiths Belt/CORBIS, 38
© Bettmann/CORBIS, 8, 31, 33, 36
© Burstein Collection/CORBIS, 5, 14
© W. Cody/CORBIS, 18
© Macduff Everton/CORBIS, 17
© Todd Gipstein/CORBIS, 11
© Catherine Karnow/CORBIS, 35
© North Wind Pictures, 7, 21, 22, 27, 28, 29, 40, 41
© Richard T. Nowitz/CORBIS, 19
© Phil Schermeister/CORBIS, 30
© Lee Snider/CORBIS, 9, 24, 42
© Paul A. Souders/CORBIS, 12

Copyright © 2002 by KidHaven Press, an imprint of Gale Group, Inc.
      P. O. Box 289009, San Diego, CA 92198-9009

Printed in the U.S.A.

Contents

Life in a New Land

On a November morning nearly four hundred years ago, a ship called the *Mayflower* dropped its anchor near the northern coast of America. The people on board crowded onto the deck, eager to see the land. Having sailed across the Atlantic Ocean from England, they had been at sea for more than three months. Now, at last, they had arrived at the New World, where they planned to begin new lives.

The land before them did not look inviting, however. In all directions they saw nothing but empty sand dunes and dark forest. Winter was coming. The **settlers** would have to make shelters quickly and find food. Here in this new place, which they named Plymouth, after the port from which they had set sail, there were no towns, roads, farms, houses, or markets. The settlers were starting from scratch.

That first year in America was terribly hard. Because of the cold, the scarcity of food, and the diseases that swept through the group, half of the settlers died. As time went on, though, the tiny **colony** grew. Babies were born. More settlers came from England and other countries, and eventually they formed thir-

A painting of the ship the *Mayflower,* which brought the Pilgrims to America.

teen colonies along the east coast of America. Over the next 150 years, the people of these colonies carved out a way of life for themselves in the American wilderness. That way of life is gone now, but many traces of it remain. From the buildings, furniture, and tools the colonists made, from the journals and letters they wrote, and from the pictures they painted, people today can get a good idea of what life was like in the early days of America.

Chapter 1

At Home

In the early years of the colonies—before ships began coming regularly from England bringing things like tools and furniture—the colonists had to make or build nearly everything they used. The first things they had to build—as soon as they arrived—were houses.

Houses

The first colonists to come to the New World made shelters that were barely houses at all. Some lived for a while in tents or caves. Others dug square pits in the ground, lined them with boards, and made a roof of bark or grass. These dwellings were not good for much but keeping out the worst of the cold, rain, and snow.

As soon as they could, the settlers looked for ways to build better houses. Back in England, their houses had often been made of brick or stone. Wood was not plentiful in England because much of the country's forests had been cut down. But in America, the forests seemed to go on forever, offering plenty of wood for building.

A typical house had one big room, measuring about twenty by twenty feet. At one end there might be a loft with a ladder leading up to it. At the other end was a fire-

The plentiful forests in America provided lumber for the colonists' homes.

place. This fireplace provided the only heat. All of the cooking was done there, too. The bathroom was always a separate shed behind the house. No matter what the weather, people went outside when they had to use it.

The walls of these houses were made of boards. The windows, if any existed, were made of oiled paper. The roof might be made of thatch—that is, bundles of dry grass tightly tied together. Or it might be made of sod—pieces of root-matted earth.

These houses were often drafty and cold. A man who visited one such house in 1697 described it as "so wretchedly constructed that if you are not so close to the fire as almost to burn yourself, you cannot keep warm, for the wind blows through everywhere."[1]

There was not much light inside, either. People burned candles for light, or if they did not have candles, they burned knots of wood from pine trees. The air inside the house was smoky from the fire, and often the floor was no more than packed-down dirt. In these rough one-room houses, families cooked, ate, and slept. There might be as many as twelve people living in one house together.

Furniture

Most of the early colonists did not bring furniture with them on the ship. They might have one trunk holding clothes and blankets, but they had no chairs, tables, or beds. In America, they made stools or benches to sit on, or they sat on their trunks.

The colonists used their fireplaces for cooking and as their only source of heat.

A re-creation of a colonial home. These houses were small, cold, and drafty.

Their beds were often just mattresses that were stuffed with corn husks or rags and were placed on the floor. In some houses the bed was a wooden frame attached to the wall with hinges at one end. In the daytime the bed could be lifted up and fastened to the wall so it was out of the way.

Tables in these early houses were very simple: They were made from one or two boards supported by trestles (like sawhorses) at either end. These boards, placed near the fire, were where the family gathered for meals.

Mealtime

When it was time to eat, the woman of the house set the table. She put a cloth over the boards and set out napkins. For plates, she put down **trenchers**, which were wooden slabs that had been hollowed into shallow bowls. Each trencher was shared by two people, who ate from it with their hands or with spoons; before the late 1600s, hardly anyone used forks.

In many homes, children were not allowed to sit down at the table; instead, they stood up to eat. Sometimes they stood behind their parents, who handed food back to them. A book from that time instructs children about proper table manners: "Sing not, hum not, wiggle not. Spit no where in the room but in the corner. . . . Eat not too fast nor with Greedy Behavior."[2]

The food was located at the center of the table in a big serving dish, usually made of **pewter**, a metal with a dull-silver color. There was also a large drinking cup, made of pewter or wood. Everyone at the table drank from the same cup, passing it from hand to hand.

Simple Meals

A meal usually consisted of just one dish. It might be a meat stew, for instance. The colonists had many kinds of meat—the woods were full of deer, wild turkeys, squirrels, rabbits, and other creatures. Likewise, the ocean and the rivers teemed with fish.

Many meals included corn. The Native Americans had taught the colonists how to grow corn when they had first arrived in the New World. The colonists made corn mush, corn bread, popcorn, corn on the cob, and used corn in soup and stew. A stew might include other vegetables, too, such as pumpkins, beans, carrots, or

In a historical re-creation, a woman in colonial dress prepares a meal.

Dinner in the colonies usually consisted of a one-dish meal served by candlelight.

peas. Blackberries and wild grapes grew in the forests, and the colonists planted fruit trees that gave them so many apples and pears that they used them in every possible way. A visitor from Sweden said in a letter home, "Apple-pie is used through the whole year, and when fresh apples are no longer to be had, dried ones are used."[3]

When a meal was over, a large basket would be passed around the table to collect napkins, trenchers, and spoons. Afterward, the table boards were taken down and put away.

Space was tight in these small, crowded houses. There might be a cupboard for small kitchen items, but there were no closets. People used trunks to store things they seldom used, and things they used often—like their clothes—they hung from pegs on the walls.

Clothes

The early colonists needed clothes that would wear well in rough conditions. Most people wore simple clothes of linen, wool, or leather. Usually they had no more than one or two complete outfits.

Men wore a heavy jacket called a **doublet**, with a shirt underneath. Their pants, called **breeches**, came just to the knees. Long stockings covered the rest of the leg.

Women wore outfits composed of three pieces: a long skirt, a **bodice** (like a vest), and separate sleeves that were tied into the armholes of the bodice. They also wore aprons over their skirts to protect against dirt and stains.

Little children, both boys and girls, wore petticoats, which were like long shirts and had what were called "hanging sleeves." These were long extra sleeves that hung from the shoulders nearly to the ground. Adults often held onto the sleeves to guide children while they

The Pilgrims wore simple clothing that had to stand up to hard work and harsh weather.

A few wealthy townspeople in the colonies wore fancy clothing from England.

were learning to walk. When children were about six years old, they were dressed in the same kinds of clothes as adults.

Some of the wealthier people who lived in towns wore fine clothing that came from England, such as silk and satin dresses and coats that were decorated with ribbons or lace. But most of the colonists were not wealthy, and such fancy clothes would have been nothing but burdens to them. The clothes they wore had to suit the way they spent their time, and most of their time was spent in hard work.

Chapter 2

At Work

People came to the New World with different skills and occupations, such as blacksmiths, potters, bakers, and fishermen. But nearly all of them, at least at first, had to do the most important work of all: producing food for their families. For the first hundred years or so of the American colonies, most settlers earned their living from the land.

The Farmer

Farming in this new land required endless hard work. Forests had to be cut down before crops could be planted. Fields were full of stones, and tools were crude and worked badly. A cold snap or a plague of caterpillars could wipe out a whole season's crop.

Even so, most farmers managed to grow enough to feed their families and have a little left over to sell. They always had a vegetable garden near the house, where they grew peas, carrots, onions, parsnips, turnips, and cabbages—the food upon which the family lived. In the outlying fields farmers grew their crops—sometimes oats, barley, or wheat but always corn. Corn was the

A re-creation of a colonial vegetable garden is pictured here.

easiest to grow and the most useful. The corn husks could be used to stuff mattresses, and the cobs could be made into pipes or bottle stoppers. And corn, of course, was excellent as food, both for people and for animals. Some of it was eaten fresh, some was dried, and some was taken to the miller to be made into cornmeal.

The Miller

The miller operated the mill, where the farmers' grains were ground into flour or meal. In the mill were two large, heavy, round stones called **millstones**. They sat one on top of the other, making what looked like an enormous stone layer cake. The wheat or corn was put between the stones, and when the upper stone turned, the grain was ground into fine bits.

Manpower was not enough to turn these millstones because they were so large and heavy and had to be turned for so long. Some mills used water power.

Millers ground grain into flour or meal using two large millstones (pictured).

Many mills used water power to turn the large millstones.

These mills were built beside fast-running streams, and the running water turned a wheel that was connected to the millstones inside. Other mills—called windmills—used wind power. The wind turned great blades on the top of the building, and the turning blades turned the millstones.

With flour and cornmeal for bread, porridge, and cakes, and with vegetables from the garden and fruit from the trees, the settlers were well supplied with food from the land. And because they all lived near the coast, they had food from the sea as well.

The Fisherman

The ocean waters off the coast of New England were rich with fish. From the beginning of colonial times, fishermen took advantage of this bounty.

Storms and rough waters, however, made the fishermen's job dangerous. Their small boats were no match for the hurricanes that sometimes swept along the coast, like the great storm of 1635, which the Pilgrim governor William Bradford described in his journal: "[It] was such a mighty storm of wind and rain as none living in these parts, either English or Indians, ever saw. . . . Divers [various] vessels were lost at sea and many more in extreme danger."[4]

Codfish is pictured drying on a line. Dried cod was an important part of the colonists' diet.

In spite of the dangers, the fishing industry flourished. Codfish, especially, was plentiful. Most of the codfish was dried and salted so that it would keep a long time. Dried codfish became an important part of the colonists' diet.

Though farm families could grow or catch most of their own food, they could not produce absolutely everything they needed. They might make their own clothes, candles, chairs, wagons, and soap, but they usually did not make the blades for their axes or the nails for their barns. For those, they turned to the blacksmith.

The Blacksmith

The blacksmith worked with iron. He softened iron bars by heating them until they were extremely hot. Then, he hammered the glowing iron and shaped it into nails and hinges and the blades for plows, axes, and hoes. He also made repairs to metal parts of wagons and guns.

A different sort of smith, called a farrier, made iron shoes for horses. When he had bent the iron to the right shape, the farrier pounded it onto the bottom of the horse's hoof with nails. The shoe kept the horse's hooves from wearing down.

The blacksmith and the farrier had to work carefully. Molten metal could cause serious burns, and the heavy tools and anvils, handled carelessly, could crush a foot or a finger. The work of the blacksmith—like so much work in the colonies—could often require the help of the doctor.

Farriers made horseshoes and nailed them onto the horse's hooves.

The Doctor

In the New World, colonists encountered all kinds of ailments—from ordinary colds to serious diseases such as **smallpox**. They were also prone to accidents because of the harsh conditions in which they lived. Therefore, they needed doctors.

Unfortunately, the doctors of the early colonies were not always effective healers. No one knew yet about the germs that cause disease and infection. Doctors did not **sterilize** the instruments they used, and often they did not even wash their hands between patients. Without realizing it, they passed infections from one patient to another.

For many ailments, doctors prescribed bleeding. They sometimes attached **leeches** to a patient's skin to

Colonial doctors lacked the scientific knowledge to be effective healers.

suck out the blood thought to be causing the problem. The results of this remedy were poor. Most of the time, bleeding left the patient weak from loss of blood.

Doctors also treated illnesses with drugs, many of which came from plants. Wild onions were supposed to be good for colds, dandelions for the bite of wild dogs, and peppermint for stomachaches. Some of these drugs were helpful. The foxglove plant, for instance, was used for patients with heart trouble; it helped the heart to beat more strongly.

Doctors of colonial times used their limited knowledge as best they could. But a great deal of the time, people who became ill or had an accident had to rely on home remedies. The person who gathered and applied these remedies was usually the housewife. Caring for the sick was one of her many jobs.

The Housewife

While the men were working on land and at sea, the women were at home doing the work that kept the whole family going.

First in importance was food. Women planted and tended the vegetable garden and preserved the harvest so it would last through the winter. They pickled all kinds of foods—not just cucumbers but also walnuts, mushrooms, lemons, and parsley. They made jams and jellies, and they salted and smoked meat. They also prepared meals for the family every day.

Women were also responsible for making the family's clothes. In many families the woman made the cloth

Colonial women's chores included tending their large gardens.

itself. Using plant fibers or tufts of wool, she would make thread with a spinning wheel. Then, she would stretch the thread on a loom—a large, complicated wooden machine that had a place in nearly every household. As she wove the thread back and forth through the loom, she gradually produced a piece of cloth. When it was finished, she could sew it into useful items such as shirts, dresses, tablecloths, petticoats, and aprons.

Women were always busy. One appreciative husband wrote,

> From early in the morning till late at night she is constantly employed in the affairs of the family . . . her cleanliness about the house, her attendance in the orchard . . . her seeing all our washing done . . .

her making of twenty large cheeses . . . besides her sewing, knitting &c[etc.]. . . . Thus she looketh well to the ways of her household, and eateth not the bread of idleness.[5]

A Life of Constant Toil

For the families of the early colonies, life was almost entirely taken up with work of one kind or another. Even the children, when they were old enough, joined their father in the fields or their mother in the kitchen or at the loom. Just about the only time not spent in farmwork or household chores were the hours when children attended school and the family went to church.

Chapter 3

At Church and at School

The colonial settlers usually built their churches close to the center of their towns. This reflected the way they felt about religion: It was close to the center of their lives. Schools, too, were important, and part of their importance had to do with religion: Children needed to learn to read so that they could read the Bible.

The Meetinghouse

The place where people attended church was usually called the meetinghouse. The citizens of a town would all come together to build it. The walls of the meetinghouse were plain wood, and the roof was topped with a short tower that housed a large bell, which was rung to call people to services on Sunday morning. Inside the meetinghouse were benches and pews—that is, seats boxed in with shoulder-high wooden walls. The windows were made of plain glass; if the congregation could not afford glass, they were made of oiled paper.

These meetinghouses were never heated, so they were very cold in winter. People came to services bundled up in their warmest clothes and huddled close together. Often they brought along foot warmers, which were small boxes containing a heated brick. Sometimes dogs were allowed to come in and warm their masters' feet by sitting on them.

Going to Meeting

Sunday church services lasted most of the day. Sermons were long, with the minister perhaps preaching for two or three hours. After the morning service people went to a "noon-house" for lunch. There, warmed by a crackling fire, they ate food that they had brought from home. Children sometimes listened to a sermon as they ate. Then, the service continued after lunch.

A Pilgrim couple walks to church, the woman carrying her Bible.

During these long church services, boys and girls often got restless. Boys, especially, caused so much disturbance that so-called inspectors of youth were appointed to keep them under control. The inspectors' job, according to a description from this period, was "to see that [the boys] behave comelie [appropriately], and to use such raps and blows as shall be meet [proper]" to keep them

27

Colonists leave church following a long day of worship.

from "Smiling and Larfing [laughing] and Intiseing [enticing] others to the same Evil."[6] They also had to keep an eye on the girls, who were apt to laugh at the antics of the boys.

Children of colonial days were expected to be quiet and diligent almost all the time. Sundays were for "going to meeting" and for quiet activities such as reading the Bible. Weekdays—at least for some children— were for paying close attention to the schoolmaster.

The Schools

Colonial schoolhouses were usually simple log buildings of only one room. If there were windows, they were more likely to be filled with oiled paper than glass.

A fireplace kept the room warm in winter; the students' parents provided the firewood. Children sat on benches or log blocks, and the teacher—one teacher for all ages—sat at the front of the room.

A class might include students as young as seven and as old as fifteen. In the summer, the school day might be as long as eight hours. In winter it was shorter. Whereas some schools ran all year, others lasted only a couple of months.

Lessons

The main subjects in colonial schools were reading and writing. Students also learned a little arithmetic. If they had a good writing teacher, they might learn the fancy penmanship that was greatly admired at the time.

A child stands quietly at church. Sometimes children became restless during long services and acted up.

A man in colonial dress sweeps a bridge leading to an old schoolhouse.

Textbooks did not exist. Students usually learned reading from something called a horn book. This was a piece of wood shaped like a paddle. On it was a sheet of paper printed with the alphabet, some syllables for reading practice (such as *ib, eb, ab*), and the Lord's Prayer. A thin piece of horn was tacked over the paper to protect it. The horn was transparent enough so that the printing on the paper showed through. The children would hold their "books" by the handle, and as the teacher pointed out letters at the front of the class, they would call out the letters' names.

Because paper and pencils were scarce, students sometimes wrote on the white bark of the birch tree. Or they might use a slate—a small square of smooth, flat stone on which they wrote with chalk.

Schoolmasters often ruled their students very strictly. Disobedient students might be whipped with a strap or made to stand in a corner wearing a dunce cap. Some teachers punished students by hanging signs on them that said such things as "Tell-Tale" and "Idle-Boy."

But there were wise teachers, too, who treated their students kindly. One such teacher, Samuel Dock, explained how he relied on rewards to encourage learning: "If [a child] can say its A.B.C.'s in order, one after the other . . . it is put into the A-b, Abs. When it gets thus far, its father must give it a penny and its mother must cook for it

Disobedient school children were punished, sometimes by being forced to wear a dunce cap.

two eggs, because of its industry; and a similar reward is due to it when it goes further into words; and so forth."[7]

A student in a school like Samuel Dock's would most likely have been a boy. Very few girls went to school. They were usually educated in a different way.

Girls' Schooling

Parents considered schooling more important for boys than for girls. Boys, after all, would be doing business out in the world; girls would be at home cooking, sewing, and cleaning.

Since it was considered important for all people to read the scriptures, parents might teach their daughters the basics of reading. One way girls learned their alphabet was by making needlework squares called **samplers.** In small, careful stitches, they would embroider letters, pictures, and short verses. A typical sampler verse went like this:

> This is my Sampler,
> Here you see
> What care my Mother
> Took of me.[8]

Sometimes very young girls went to so-called dame schools, which were usually run by a woman from her home. There, a few children—both boys and girls— learned their alphabet and some biblical stories. Then, at about age seven, boys would go on to the school- house, and girls would go home to learn the skills of a housewife. Those girls who lived in cities and came

Children at a "dame school," run by a colonial woman in her home.

from wealthy families might continue in a dame school for a few more years, learning reading and writing and maybe a little music or drawing. But even girls from prominent families often received no schooling at all. "I never was sent to any school,"[9] wrote the wife of America's second president, John Adams.

All Work and No Play

Life in colonial America was so full of duties—work, church, school—that little time was left for enjoyment. But even in the difficult early days, the colonists did allow themselves some pleasures.

Chapter 4

Amusements

For the early colonists, who spent so much time laboring on their isolated farms, the best amusements were times when they gathered with others. Groups of people found ways to have fun even while they worked.

Work Made into Fun

Women's work could be tedious and lonely. A woman might spend hours by herself working on a quilt, for instance, or paring apples. But on neighboring farms, other women were doing the same kinds of work. So sometimes women gathered at one house and did their work together. These gatherings, called **bees**, were both useful and enjoyable.

The quilting bee was one of the most popular gatherings. Women came from miles around to spend time together making quilts for their beds. First, they took scraps of material left over from other uses—dresses, shirts, aprons, curtains—and cut them into small, neat pieces. They sewed these pieces together in patterns. Many of these patterns had names that described them: rising sun, log cabin, love knot, and Chinese puzzle. When they would finish two blanket-size patchwork

Colonial women sometimes found their unending chores to be boring and lonely.

sheets, they would stretch these on a wooden frame with a layer of padding between them. Next, they would raise the frame onto chairs or tables and sit around the four sides and stitch the layers together. As they worked, they talked and laughed. They might make one quilt or many quilts in their time together. A quilting bee could last for days.

Gatherings could also center around other kinds of work. Women might come together in the fall for an apple-paring bee. They might also gather for a spinning bee or a knitting bee. All of these bees gave colonial women a chance to talk with their neighbors and get work done at the same time.

Not all work gatherings were just for women. Whole families gathered for barn raisings, where the building of a new barn would be followed by a feast and maybe a dance on the new barn floor. In the fall, people often had corn-husking parties. After they had picked the ears of corn and tossed them in large piles, neighbors sat together and tore the husks from the ears. Most of the corn had yellow kernels, but a few had colored kernels—orange, black, red. According to

A colonial tradition is pictured here in this 1970 barn raising.

tradition, any man who found an ear with red kernels could ask for a kiss from his sweetheart.

Although adults had so little free time that they had to combine their fun with work, children—especially young ones—had time for pure fun.

Children's Games

Some of the games played by colonial children are the same ones that children play today. Boys practiced archery, played marbles, and flew kites. Girls jumped rope and played hopscotch and hide-and-seek.

Other games of the time are less familiar. Boys played a game called one-oh-cat, for instance. They drove a stake into the ground and balanced a stick on top of it. One boy hit the stick with a bat and sent it flying as high as possible. Other boys tried to catch it as it came down, and if they did, the hitter was out.

A book called *The Pretty Little Pocket Book*, written in colonial times, gives instructions for children's games in short rhymes. A game called chuck farthing, for example, in which boys tossed pennies into a hole, is explained like this:

As you value your Pence
At the Hole take your Aim.
Chuck all safely in,
And You'll win the Game.[10]

Singing games were popular, too. Just as little children do today, colonial children played ring-around-a-rosy and London Bridge is falling down. They also played counting-out games, in which one child would stand in the center of a circle of children and point at each person while saying a rhyme. The child being pointed at when the rhyme ended was out, and the counting continued until only one person—the winner—was left.

Toys

Colonial children had few toys, especially in the early years of America. If they did have toys, they were home-made because few families had the money to buy them.

A girl might have a doll made from rags or corn husks. A boy might make himself a whistle or a wind-mill with his jack knife. Parents, if they had time, might carve a hobby horse for a young child or make a top or a pair of ice skates.

A woman creates a doll from corn husks, in the style of dolls from colonial times.

Sometimes religious beliefs determined what toys children could have. The Quakers, for instance, did not approve of any sort of fancy dress or decoration, which they believed distracted people from the true service of God. They wore very plain clothes in neutral colors such as gray and brown. When one young Quaker girl received a doll from France as a gift, her mother took off the doll's stylish pink dress and made a plain gray dress for her instead.

Other kinds of amusements were also restricted by religion, especially in the Puritan colonies, where the church elders believed that people should spend their time working hard and doing good deeds. Having fun was all right as long as it was useful, virtuous fun, and as long as there was not too much of it. Some kinds of fun, however, were not allowed.

Dancing and Singing

Dancing was allowed but not encouraged. Men and women, however, could not dance with each other, and organized dances were against the law. In 1681, when a French dancing master came to Boston to set up a dancing school, the town governors shut down his school.

There were rules about singing, too, especially in church. The Puritans sang Bible verses in their church services, but the purpose was to praise God, not to make beautiful sounds. People who visited Puritan church services sometimes commented on the unpleasant, confused sound of their singing.

The religious Puritans frowned on dancing and the singing of songs other than hymns.

Outside of church there was more tuneful singing. At social gatherings and work parties, people often sang old ballads that had been passed down through the years. Most of these were songs from the home countries of the colonists—England, Scotland, and Ireland. Many of them, such as "Barb'ra Allen," are still sung today:

In Scarlet town where I was born,
There was a fair maid dwellin'
Made every youth cry Well-a-day,
Her name was Barb'ra Allen.[11]

During the 1700s, people began writing songs and publishing them as **broadsides**—that is, sheets of paper that were pinned up on walls and handed out on street corners. These were the popular songs of the day, and many of them were based on current events. This is a verse from a song of the Revolutionary War:

> Fight on America's noble sons,
> Fear not Britannia's thundering guns;
> Maintain your cause from year to year,
> God's on your side, you need not fear.[12]

The old-fashioned Puritans sometimes disapproved of these songs, but people sang them anyway.

Changing Times

As time passed, life in the American colonies grew less harsh and difficult. People no longer had to spend every moment just surviving. Religious groups such as the Puritans relaxed their rigid rules somewhat. Churches rang with real singing and the playing of instruments.

People enjoyed dancing and other amusements as the Puritans became less strict in their ways.

A faithful reproduction of a pilgrim village, located at Plimouth Plantation, a living history museum in Plymouth, Massachusetts.

There were dances, concerts, and theater performances. The colonists—who were soon to be citizens of a new country, the United States of America—could come together not just to share their labor but to share their joy and playfulness as well.

Notes

Chapter One: At Home

1. Quoted in David Freeman Hawke, *Everyday Life in Colonial America.* New York: Harper and Row, 1988, p. 49.
2. Quoted in Alice Morse Earle, *Home and Child Life in Colonial Days.* Ed. Shirley Glubok. New York: Macmillan, 1969, p. 53.
3. Quoted in Earle, *Home and Child Life in Colonial Days,* p. 81.

Chapter Two: At Work

4. Quoted in "Chronicles of the Pilgrim Fathers," Bibliomania.com. (http://lternet.edu/hfr/data/hf011/reports.html).
5. Quoted in Alice Morse Earle, *Colonial Dames and Good Wives.* New York: Frederick Ungar, 1962, p. 259.

Chapter Three: At Church and at School

6. Quoted in George F. Willison, *Saints and Strangers.* New York: Time, 1964, p. 398.
7. Quoted in Hawke, *Everyday Life in Colonial America,* p. 136.
8. Quoted in Hawke, *Everyday Life in Colonial America,* p. 222.
9. Quoted in Hawke, *Everyday Life in Colonial America,* p. 123.

Chapter Four: Amusements

10. Quoted in Earle, *Home and Child Life in Colonial Days,* p. 347.
11. Quoted in "Popular Songs in American History," Contemplator.com. (http://www.contemplator.com/america/index.html).
12. Quoted in "Popular Songs in American History."

Glossary

bee: a get-together combining work and pleasure, such as a quilting bee or an apple-paring bee

bodice: part of a colonial woman's clothing—a vest to which sleeves were attached

breeches: Pants worn by colonial men; they came only to the knee.

broadside: a song or verse written on a single sheet of paper and posted in public places

colony: A place settled by people who come from elsewhere and who are still governed by the country from which they came.

doublet: a man's jacket

leeches: a kind of worm that sucks blood

millstones: The large flat stones in a mill; when they turn, they rub against each other and grind the grain between them.

pewter: a metal with a dull silver color

samplers: pieces of cloth on which girls demonstrated their skill in needlework

settlers: people who left their homes and settled in a new land

smallpox: a serious disease that causes fever and blisters on the skin

sterilize: to make something very clean, usually by heating it, so that disease-causing microorganisms are destroyed

trenchers: Wooden plates; two people usually shared one trencher.

For Further Exploration

Books

Alice Morse Earle, *Home and Child Life in Colonial Days*. Ed. Shirley Glubok. New York: Macmillan, 1969. An illustrated book covering all aspects of colonial home life.

Leonard Everett Fisher, *Colonial Craftsmen: The Doctors*. New York: Benchmark Books, Marshall Cavendish, 1997. A book about the doctors, diseases, and medicines of colonial times.

Lucille Recht Penner, *Eating the Plates: A Pilgrim Book of Food and Manners*. New York: Macmillan, 1991. An interesting, humorously written book about food, cooking, and eating, including illustrations and some colonial recipes.

Victoria Sherrow, *Huskings, Quiltings, and Barn Raisings: Work-Play Parties in Early America*. New York: Walker, 1992. This book discusses the different ways in which colonial Americans enjoyed themselves.

Bernardine S. Stevens, *Colonial American Craftspeople*. New York: Franklin Watts, 1993. This book offers detailed descriptions of the work of different kinds of craftspeople, including woodworkers, papermakers, metalworkers, dressmakers, and leather workers.

Websites

Colonial Williamsburg
(www.history.org/almanack.htm). A beautifully
illustrated site that lets you take a tour of colonial
Williamsburg. There are sections on buildings,
tradespeople, families, food, gardening, and clothing—a comprehensive and very informative site.

Daily Life in 1621 (http://teacher.scholastic.com/
thanksgiving/plimoth/daily.htm). This interesting
site compares the lifestyle of the Pilgrims with the
lifestyle of the Wampanoag, the Indians who lived in
North America when the Pilgrims arrived. Pictures
and text show the differences between their clothes,
their food, their houses, and other aspects of their
lives.

Education World
(www.educationworld.com/a_sites/sites011.shtml).
This is a list of sites having to do with colonial
America. Among others, there is a site about colonial
Williamsburg, one about Old Sturbridge Village, and
one on soapmaking.

Perspectives on Liberty (www.pbs.org/ktca/liberty/
perspectives/dailylife.html). This site shows a painting of a colonial scene. Clicking on parts of the picture brings up information about that aspect of
colonial life.

Popular Songs in American History (www.contemplator.
com/america/index.html). Here you can listen to
dozens of songs and tunes from colonial America.
Information is provided about each one.

Index